FORGIVENESS
SPEAKS VOLUMES
7 STEPS TO FORGIVENESS

Shonté Foster

FORGIVENESS SPEAKS VOLUMES: 7 Steps To Forgiveness
Copyright © 2019 by Shonté Foster & Sent2Heal Ministries

All rights reserved. Written permission from the author must be secured to use or reproduce any part of this book except for brief quote in critical reviews or articles. Author must be given credit for all quotes used.

Unless otherwise indicated, all Scripture marked KJV quotations are taken from are taken from the KING JAMES VERSION (KJV): KING JAMES VERSION, public domain.

Scripture quotations marked MSG are taken from THE MESSAGE, copyright © 1993, 2002, 2018 by Eugene H. Peterson. Used by permission of NavPress. All rights reserved. Represented by Tyndale House Publishers, Inc.

ISBN (978-164467066-8)

Printed in USA by Digital Print & Imaging (www.dpilr.com)

TABLE OF CONTENTS

FOREWORD	*7*
INTRODUCTION	*9*
STEP ONE: DECISION DAY	*11*
STEP TWO: FORGIVING FOR REAL!	*15*
STEP THREE: FORGETTING FOREVER!	*21*
STEP FOUR: FAITH FOR FORGIVING	*25*
STEP FIVE: GUARDING GRACE	*31*
STEP SIX: THINKING RIGHT THOUGHTS!	*37*
STEP SEVEN: GIVING AND GETTING	*41*
ADDENDUM: FORGIVING SELF	*45*
ADENDUM: FORGIVING GOD	*51*
CONCLUSION	*55*

FOREWORD

This book is a message of hope and freedom.

Negative experiences, hostile environments, or adversarial encounters lead individuals to harbor unforgiveness towards others or even themselves.

7 Steps to Forgiveness is formatted so that those held captive by these past or present pains can receive revelation and Bible-based instructions. Readers will learn how to be set free. Therefore, they will not carry that same incapacitating pain into their futures.

Wounds, scars, and hurts created by offense - and the accompanying un-forgiveness - can leave people in a state of haplessness, helplessness and, worst of all, hopelessness. It is an entangling, ensnaring snare from which one can only be sprung free by the grace and power of God.

Through divine revelation, Shonte' Foster, has masterfully captured the root causes of unforgiveness. She skillfully addresses each issue by sharing spiritual principles, specific precepts, and step-by-step processes for being released into inner healing and deliverance.

This book, 7 Steps to Forgiveness, will help you walk victoriously and triumphantly in life as you learn how, and decide to walk the path of forgiveness.

INTRODUCTION

Sometimes our hurts and pains seem as large as mountains and can feel just as insurmountable. But there is a way out of that pain, and it has been made available to us through the word of God. In Mark Chapter 11, Jesus tells his disciples that they have the power to speak to the mountain, command it to be moved into the sea, and it would obey them. He didn't say it might obey, he said it would. It sounds so wonderful! All that is necessary to move a MOUNTAIN of pain and free our emotions from years of torment is SPEAKING to it. Then we read verse 25, and realize there is an addendum, *"While you stand praying—FORGIVE".*

The question becomes how? At some point you've been told you must forgive, but no one tells you how. It is usually said like this: *"You just need to forgive them."* And when you ask, *"How do I do that?"* the answer is, *"You just do it."* This 7-step guide to forgiveness is designed to answer the "how to" question and help you to understand the "why" as well.

Most areas of our lives can heal and grow by starting from a place of forgiveness. True forgiveness can alter the course of the human condition by healing racial issues, political divides, broken marriages, sibling rivalries, parent-child relationships, business partnerships, and the list goes on.

I have been teaching an *8-Steps to Inner-healing and Deliverance* program for more than 10 years and, with each new group, the step that causes the biggest stir is the same: forgiveness.

Often, I've been urged to teach forgiveness as its own separate program. That's why I've written this book. Since forgiveness is needed in so many areas of life, this book is the first of many in an effort to answer that call.

Although *Forgiveness Speaks Volumes* is written in seven steps, this is by no means intended to be a one-week process. Forgiveness is a process and a journey. You should set aside time daily to actively walk through this process, journaling as you go.

Let's Get Started!

STEP ONE: DECISION DAY

Forgiving starts with a simple decision. A decision is the act of making up one's mind. I know that I used the word "simple" when describing the type of decision that is needed to forgive; however, backing up your decision and staying with it, regardless of the emotions that arise, can be anything but simple. You must be determined to stay with the process of forgiving until your emotions have completely healed and the painful memories have faded.

Many people see forgiving as a one-time event (meaning they can simply say *"I forgive"* and it will be over) but forgiving is a process of healing.

I like to compare this process to that of a broken bone. If a person broke a leg and went into the emergency room to have it repaired, the doctor would x-ray the leg, determine the condition of the bone, set it, and place it in a cast to hold it steady until it heals. The person with the injury would not expect to be *"back to normal"* immediately upon receiving the cast. They would expect to wear the cast for 6-12 weeks and walk with crutches until the bone is properly healed. If he or she were to leave and take the cast right off, the bone would *not* be held steady until properly restored.

In the same way, just saying *"I forgive"* will not cause your emotions to heal. It only starts the process. The process must be maintained for true healing to take place. *Deciding to forgive* and saying, *"I forgive,"* places your injured part (your emotions) into the cast, which gets you off to a great start.

During this time of forgiving, the goal is to stay in the process until each step is completed. Then, repeat as needed.

Make up your mind to forgive today!

- **Decision** - The act of deciding or making up one's mind; the quality of being positive and firm; determination.

- **Scripture reading:** Mark 11:11-25

Forgiveness Speaks Volumes *7 Steps to Forgiveness*

NOTES

Make a list of what/who you will forgive today.

_____

_____

_____

_____

_____

How can you apply the scripture reading?

_____

_____

_____

_____

_____

PRAYER

Father, I know that your word says while we stand praying forgive. Therefore, I have decided to forgive everyone and everything that is listed above. I ask you to remind me of anything or anyone else that needs to be added to this list and I ask that you help me to support my decision by staying with it until my heart and emotions are fully restored. I say out of my mouth that I forgive today. I will continue to say that I forgive until it fully manifests. I will have what I say.

In Jesus' Name I pray, Amen!

NOTES

STEP TWO: FORGIVING FOR REAL!

"If I forgive them, they will get away
with what they did to me."

"I don't want it to look like I approve of what they did."

"If I forgive them, I'll have to return to the relationship."

The list can go on and on. Many times, we attempt to make up our minds to forgive, but our own thoughts get in the way. We have preconceived ideas about what forgiveness really is. To be clear let's look at a few definitions.

- **Forgive** - To grant pardon for or remission of something; cease to demand the penalty for; To remit as a debt.

- **Forgive (Greek)** *aphiemi* pronounced **af-ee-ay-me** - to send away or to let be.

- **Debt/Trespass - (Greek)** *opheile* pronounced **of-i-lay** - what is owed.

- **Forget** - to be unable to recall something previously known to the mind; to fail or cease to remember. To lose interest in or regard for; overlook purposefully, disregard.

With these definitions is mind, let's talk about what forgiveness is not.

Forgiving is not condoning what the person did or said. It is not returning to a harmful relationship. It is not becoming a doormat for another person to walk on. In some cases, there may be full reconciliation of relationships (when it's healthy to do so). But that in no way is the proof of forgiveness.

You may say, *"What is forgiveness then?"* I like the Greek definition—to send it away. It implies that if you do not forgive, it stays with you. Regardless of how horrible or how small the thing may have been, (murder, rape, incest, betrayal, lies or slander) it stays with you until it is sent away.

Since the goal in forgiving is the removal of hurt and pain within one's self, we must not focus on whether the other person is deserving or not. In fact, forgiving isn't done for the other person at all. Forgiveness is done for you the forgiver. Our focus must remain on the process of healing self. I am forgiving to heal me. My focus in this process of letting go is not to let *THEM* off the hook. It is to let *ME* recover. When I cease to demand a penalty, (even if it's just an apology), I begin to heal. I'm in the process.

Forgiveness is letting go of every hurtful thing that was ever done to me or said about me without requiring any form of payment from the offender. It is sending it all away from me that I might be free.

- **Scripture reading:** Matthew 6:9-15

NOTES

Which definitions stood out to you more and why?

_____

_____

_____

_____

_____

How can you reshape your thoughts about forgiveness?

_____

_____

_____

_____

_____

PRAYER

Father your word says to forgive, and I will be forgiven.
Help me to focus on my own healing during this process and not the person or thing being forgiven. I trust you with my healing process for I know that it is you who restores my soul.
I thank you for giving me a forgiving heart.
I choose to forgive others their trespasses against me.
In Jesus' Name I pray, Amen.

NOTES

NOTES

STEP THREE: FORGETTING FOREVER!

- **Forget** - To lose interest in or regard for; overlook on purpose, disregard.

"If you knew what was done to me, you would know that there is NO way I could ever FORGET."
"I will forgive them, but I'll never forget what they did to me."

I have heard this stated many times and you may have as well. What they are really saying is, "I never intend to stay with the process of forgiveness until I fully heal. I will continue to on purpose look behind *not* ahead."

A large part of forgiving is deciding to forget (overlook on purpose) what was done. We must be willing to let it go. Let it completely fade from the forefronts of our minds.

Using the delete button is one of the best things you can do. This type of forgetting that is required in forgiveness isn't amnesia. You are not expected to forget the incident but to release/forgive the pain associated with it. You are expected to focus so fully on what is ahead of you in this healing process that you lose sight of the things that have harmed you in the past.

The Apostle Paul said in Philippians Chapter 3, "This one thing I do, forgetting those things that are behind, and reaching forth unto those things which are before. I press toward the mark…"

Pressing forward to reach any goal requires that you forget. Let go of what is behind you. It must become the "one thing" or the most important thing that you do.

Have you ever tried to drive a vehicle forward while turning and looking behind you? It is quite difficult isn't it? The outcome is usually not a good one either.

It is human nature to move in the direction you are looking. Therefore, we cannot continue looking behind us – at what was done to us – and expect to move forward into a good future. That means you can't keep going over old history and pave a road for a bright future ahead. Yes, your future is bright.

You must lose interest in what was done to you. Forgive!

- **Scripture reading:** Philippians 3:13-14; Isaiah 43:17-21 (MSG)

NOTES

How has this definition on forgetting changed your thoughts on forgiveness?

_____
_____
_____
_____
_____

How can you apply the scripture reading?

_____
_____
_____
_____
_____

PRAYER
I have chosen to forgive and forget all negative actions and words toward me. I know that I won't cease to remember the events, but I can cease to remember the accompanying pain.
I open my heart to your forgiveness process.
In Jesus' Name I pray, Amen.

NOTES

STEP FOUR: FAITH FOR FORGIVING

It is a natural reflex when you are offended or wronged to express it with your emotions. God gave us emotions as a part of our alerting and guidance system. We use our emotions (feelings) to express all aspects of what we are experiencing throughout our day. Whether our mood is high or low, we use our feelings to express it. We cry, laugh, sing, dance, scream.

When something happens and we get our feelings hurt, we often don't know how to quickly recover. We may know that we need to forgive in order to return to our norm, but we usually wait to *feel* like it. Forgiveness, however, isn't done with the feelings. The feelings are the part of us that has become wounded and can't be trusted to operate normally.

In Luke Chapter 17, Jesus talks to his disciples about offense and forgiveness. He reveals to them how important it is to keep a forgiving heart. He paints the picture of someone offending them again and again, up to seven times in one day. To their shock, they are still required to forgive that person—repeatedly. In another text, he says you must forgive not just seven times, but up to seventy times seven. He wasn't literally saying count 490 times, then you're off the hook. He was saying, you must always be willing to forgive as many times as is necessary. Upon hearing this, the disciples exclaim, "Lord increase our faith!"

They understood what is often missed: forgiveness is not something we do with our emotions. It must be done with our FAITH.

You're probably thinking "Lord increase my faith too!" Well, God has answered your prayer. According to Romans 10:17, faith comes by hearing and hearing by the word of God. Romans 12:3, says God has given to everyone the measure of faith. That means God freely gives us the faith we need to forgive as we hear His word again and again. God's word is the container of faith.

In addition, Jesus (the word himself) has already provided full payment of all sin. When he shed his blood for us on Calvary's cross, he covered all areas of forgiveness. Prior to the cross we had to forgive other's trespasses against us before we could be forgiven (Matthew 6:15). After Christ's shed blood, we forgive because we have been forgiven. When we accepted Jesus as Savior, we received a full deposit of forgiveness.

Now, as you plan out your forgiving strategy, find scriptures that teach on forgiveness and begin to meditate on them and speak them daily. This will increase your faith to forgive. Then, draw on Christ's forgiveness that was already deposited within you. As you continue to use your faith to forgive your *FEELINGS* will eventually *CATCH UP* with your *FAITH*.

Forgiveness isn't natural it is supernatural. You must connect with the supernatural God to forgive.

- **Scripture reading:** Luke 17:1-10; Romans 12:3; 10:17

NOTES

List scripture that you will use to grow your faith to forgive.

_____

_____

_____

_____

_____

How will you manage your emotions/feelings as you wait on them to catch up to your faith?

_____

_____

_____

_____

_____

PRAYER

Father, thank you for the faith that you have already deposited into my heart as your child. I choose to grow my faith my confessing and mediating your word. I know that faith comes by hearing your word continuously. I will make it a part of my daily routine. I will use my faith to forgive and my feeling will soon match my faith.
In Jesus' Name I pray, Amen.

NOTES

NOTES

STEP FIVE: GUARDING GRACE!

- **Forgiving is active not passive.**

You must be an active participant in your forgiveness process. Proverbs 4:23 says, "Guard your heart above all else for it determines the course of your life." Guarding your heart from offenses and keeping out unforgiveness can be a full-time job until you become skilled at it.

"Guard" means to watch over in order to protect or control. But what does it look like to guard your heart?

As we continue reading Proverbs 4, we get clues as to how this is achieved. Verse 24 says, "Avoid all perverse talk; stay away from corrupt speech." This is vitally important as it is human nature to do the opposite when one is offended.

Our first tendency is to talk about it to someone – and not just to one someone. Then, we repeat the offense over and over to anyone who will listen until we become emotionally drained. When we react in this manner, we are helping the offense to take root in our hearts and deepening the wound.

Your heart must be protected from things that will try to take root and spring up. This is done the way one tends to a vegetable garden. Weeds must be uprooted and kept out and so must critters that will creep in to eat the precious produce.

The mouth and the ears are two gateways into the heart. Just as our faith grows as we hear God's word, the converse is true; the more we hear and say the offense the weaker our resolve to forgive becomes. So, one of the ways we guard our hearts is to guard our mouth; another is to guard our ears.

That means it's best not to talk about what happened, unless we are talking to the person who hurt us in an effort to resolve it. We shouldn't listen to others rehearse the offense either.

Think of a time when a coworker witnessed something offensive that was said to you. Instead of squashing it, they may have responded by attempting to incite it further.

"I heard what she said to you, that wasn't called for." And it can spin out of control from there.

The best response is, "I chose to overlook that, and I'd rather not talk about it." Guarding your heart must be active, intentional, and done immediately.

According to Matthew 12:35, good things happen in your life because they spring forth from the good treasure that is stored up in your heart.

It is my job to keep my treasury good. I must tend my garden regularly to ensure that my life continues to flow in the direction I want it to go. To keep my future bright, I must maintain a forgiving heart.

- **Guard –** To watch over in order to protect or control
- **Scripture Reading:** Proverbs 4:23-27; Matthew 12:34-37

NOTES

How does the scripture reading apply to forgiveness?

_____

_____

_____

_____

_____

What behavior will you change in order to guard your heart?

_____

_____

_____

_____

PRAYER

Father, thank you for teaching me to guard my heart above all else. I will on purpose tend to the garden of my heart and pull up weeds quickly. I will keep my treasure good by keeping my conversations good. Thank you for helping me to cultivate a forgiving heart.

In Jesus' Name I pray, Amen.

NOTES

NOTES

STEP SIX: THINKING RIGHT THOUGHTS!

Another part of guarding your heart is policing your thoughts. A thought may cross your mind but that doesn't mean you should think on it. You can choose what you allow to occupy such precious real estate.

Thoughts do matter. Realize that "I" can have control. I can think thoughts on purpose and for purpose. I can cast down negative thoughts even if it really happened to me or was said about me. My mind is too valuable to waste space on negativity.

II Corinthians 10:5 commands us to *cast* (violently hurl) down *vain* (serving no purpose) imaginations and to capture every thought before it becomes a strong fortress in our minds. I love how the Message translation says we are to fit every loose thought, emotion, and impulse into a life shaped by Christ.

It is up to us to be the policemen of our thought lives. We must remain vigilant and on our guard.

In Philippian 4:8, the Apostle Paul lets us know that we can give our minds an assignment. We are not doomed to think whatever stray, negative impulse that crosses our thought path. He says, "Whatever things are true, whatever things are noble, whatever things are just, whatever things are pure, whatever things are lovely …think on these things."

This strongly indicates, that you do have a choice in the matter. Think thoughts on purpose. FORGIVE.

- **Scripture reading:** Philippians 4:8; Proverbs 23:7

NOTES

How do you handle negative memories that surface?

___

How can you apply the scripture reading to your thought life and self-talk?

___

PRAYER
Father, I confess today that I have the mind of Christ and hold the thoughts, feelings and purposes of his heart. I renew my mind in your word daily. I purpose to fill my mind with and meditate on things true, noble, reputable, authentic, compelling, gracious — the best not the worst; the beautiful not the ugly; things to praise not to curse.
In Jesus' Name, Amen.

NOTES

STEP SEVEN: GIVING AND GETTING!

Isaiah 61:3
To console those who mourn in Zion,
To give them beauty for ashes,
The oil of joy for mourning,
The garment of praise for the spirit of heaviness;
That they may be called trees of righteousness,
The planting of the Lord, that He may be glorified.

In Isaiah 61:3, God offers us His exchange program. I like to call it, "The Great Exchange." He promises to impart "Great Gifts" for our souls; to give us true, inner healing. However, these gifts are conditional. We must be willing to give up our ashes to get His beauty; give up the things that we mourn over to get His joy; and let go of the heaviness to be clothed in His beautiful garment of praise.

These conditions aren't to force us to earn these great gifts, but so the healing will be lasting. God just doesn't want this to be a temporary fix like many things in this world.

As you pray in the Spirit, God will give you practical ways to let go of your ashes. For example, in my *Sent2Heal Inner Healing and Deliverance* sessions, we do an exercise called "Write It Out." This is where you write it all on paper (getting it out of you), burn the sheets of paper, and symbolically give God the ashes. Another is called "Write It To."

This is where you write letters to the offenders (sending it away). Some feel lead to mail them, most don't.

As you walk out your forgiveness process together with God, He will lead you. He wishes above all else that you prosper and be in health as your soul prospers. (III John 2) Forgiveness prospers the soul.

It is God's desire that you have beautiful things in life, that you are filled with joy and that you are praise dancing in style!
But God is a gentleman. He will not FORCE His desires upon you. There must be a true EXCHANGE. His BEST for your WORST.

This requires that you let go (let completely drop to the ground) the ugly ashes of past hurts, the bitterness that robs you of joy, and the heavy memories that bring depression.

Then you will receive BEAUTY, JOY AND PRAISE! It's ALL up to YOU. Give to Get!

Make the Great Exchange today. FORGIVE!

- **Scripture reading**: Isaiah 61:1-7; 3 John 2

NOTES

What are you still holding on to?

_____

_____

_____

_____

_____

How can you apply the scripture reading?

_____

_____

_____

_____

_____

PRAYER

Father, I give you my Ashes today (list them).
I choose to leave them with you,
to never return to the pain of them again.
I receive your beauty, your oil of joy, and your garment of praise.
Thank you for causing my soul to prosper as I forgive.
In Jesus' Name I pray, Amen.

NOTES

ADDENDUM: FORGIVING SELF

Isaiah 61:7
For your shame you shall have double...

Joshua 2:18
When we come into the land, you must leave this *scarlet rope* hanging from the window through which you let us down. And all your family members—your father, mother, brothers, and all your relatives— must be here inside the house.

Shame is often the result of not forgiving yourself. But for your shame you shall receive double. If you master the art of forgiving yourself, God will double you! It is okay to mess up, get up, let go, and move forward. Heaven will applaud you and releases the double as long as you don't stay in the mess.

Rahab, the harlot found in the book of Joshua, exemplifies this very concept. She moves pass the shame of her past (prostitution) to not only save the lives of her entire family, but to marry one of the spies that was sent out against her doomed city and becomes the mother of the most famous husband in the bible (Boaz).

Giving herself a clean slate allowed this female, gentile, harlot, to be named in the lineage of Jesus—being placed right up there alongside the Virgin Mary. As if that wasn't enough, God uses her life as an allegory, painting a vivid picture of what he would do in the earth through His only Son thousands of years later.

The scarlet cord that she placed in the window – which caused her entire family to be saved – first points back to the exodus from Egypt. It reminds of forty years earlier when God caused the death angel to pass over the

Israelites saving them while all the first-born sons of the Egyptians were killed.

Next, it points forward to the redeeming power of the blood of Jesus that would be shed on the cross to save the World (John 3:16).

Then God uses her marriage to a Hebrew man to point forward again, illustrating how he would merge the gentiles with the Jews to make one people group (the Church, Ephesians 2:11-16).

Lastly, it points back to the promise God made in the garden to use what was hidden in woman to redeem mankind (crush the head of Satan).

Her son, Boaz, becomes a kinsman redeemer for Ruth (another picture of the Christ, the Virgin Mary's son, who would redeem all mankind). He then becomes the great, grandfather of King David, which is how they become named in the lineage of Jesus.

I believe God took the time to so thoroughly weave the tapestry of Rahab's life-story – pointing back and pointing forwarding repeatedly – to help us understand his ability to cover our past and our future. He wanted us to know that we can trust Him to make use of the good, the bad, and the ugly, if we give them to Him.

All of this is done through one woman who chose to forgive herself and move forward.

Rahab couldn't have imagined all that God would do with her broken pieces and neither can you. When you forgive yourself the possibilities for your life become boundless. You set yourself up for The Double! Apply the blood of Jesus today and forgive YOU!

- **Scripture reading:** Joshua 2

NOTES

In what areas do you need a clean slate?

NOTES

NOTES

ADENDUM: FORGIVING GOD

Are you mad at God?

Loss is one of those things that can cause anger towards God. I call it the "blame game."

"GOD, WHERE WERE YOU!?" It could be the death of a loved one, loss of marriage or maybe loss of property from a storm. Ultimately, since God is sovereign, He gets the blame.

This can be very tricky to navigate seeing that God is the very one we need to help us recover. It is the goal of Satan to blame loss on God so we will run from God instead of to Him.

God never promised us that our loved ones would live forever. However, 1Thessalonians 4:13-16, lets us know that those who died in Christ, we will see again. So, when we grieve, it won't be a long lasting, hopeless, grief. We can always lean to the hope of "till we meet again."

Another erroneous belief is that storms or other natural disasters are caused by God. The book of Job records the first "storm" as a whirlwind that killed all of Job's children. This was caused by Satan, not God. According to the law of first mention, that means every subsequent storm in life is authored by Satan. God uses them for our good but, He does not cause them to happen.

Since time doesn't heal all wounds BUT God does, a CHOICE to forgive God and release your anger towards Him puts you on the path to healing.

Forgive God Today. He's waiting with open arms.

I offer a more in-depth teaching on this subject in Sent2Heal's 8-Steps to Inner healing and Deliverance program.

NOTES

What are you angry with God about?

___

How can you use the 7 steps to forgiveness to release it?

___

NOTES

CONCLUSION

Revelation 13:8
...the Lamb slain from the foundation of the world.

John 20:22-23 (MSG)
Then he took a deep breath and breathed into them. "Receive the Holy Spirit," he said. "If you forgive someone's sins, they're gone for good. If you don't forgive sins, what are you going to do with them?"

In every relationship – whether spousal, parental, siblings, coworkers, church members, neighbors, or friends – friction will arise. Offenses will come. The best strategy is to have a plan.

Just like we plan escape routes for storms or fires and pick a meeting place for the family, we can plan an escape for offense and decide ahead of time to meet at the place of forgiveness. We can predetermine to have a forgiving heart.

The Greek definition for offense (*skandalon*) is "the trigger of a trap." Satan planned in offense to trap us. But God planned to forgive mankind before the first bite of the forbidden fruit. Before Adam could blame Eve and Eve could blame the serpent, God had planned their way out: forgiveness.

In Revelation 13:8, we learn the Lamb (Jesus) was slain before the world began. If God Almighty planned ahead to cover offenses, shouldn't We?

God PLANNED. He knew offenses would come and the relationship would be jeopardized. God planned in forgiveness. It cost him a very high price, the blood of His only son, but the benefit was many sons and daughters—family.

There are many benefits to following the plan of forgiveness. Not only is it the best way to press reset, but forgiveness can be likened to a time machine. It allows you to go back to a painful, past event, and remove the sting of it as if it never occurred.

Conveying the plan of forgiveness was so important that one of the first things that Jesus says to His disciples upon rising from the grave is, "If you forgive someone's sins, they're gone for good. If you don't forgive sins, what are you going to do with them?" (John 20:23, MSG).

To make forgiveness available to ALL, Jesus was willing to sacrifice his very life. It was His secret weapon to defeat

Satan. As soon as that weapon was deployed, He appeared to His disciples and shared it with them.

Let's continue to deploy our weapon of forgiveness by:

- Deciding to forgive (making up your mind).
- Forgiving for real (understanding what forgiveness is).
- Forgetting (overlooking on purpose).
- Building Faith to forgive (meditating God's word on forgiveness).
- Guarding your heart (watching your words).
- Thinking right thoughts (policing your thought life).
- Giving to Get (making an exchange with God).

Remember to repeat as needed. There may be times when old offenses will try to resurface. Just start at the beginning and walk back through each step.

God is partnering with you in this process, so you'll always win!

NOTES

CONCLUDING THOUGHTS?

FORGIVENESS JOURNAL

FORGIVENESS JOURNAL

FORGIVENESS JOURNAL

FORGIVENESS JOURNAL

FORGIVENESS JOURNAL

FORGIVENESS JOURNAL

FORGIVENESS JOURNAL

FORGIVENESS JOURNAL

FORGIVENESS JOURNAL

FORGIVENESS JOURNAL

FORGIVENESS JOURNAL

FORGIVENESS JOURNAL

FORGIVENESS JOURNAL

FORGIVENESS JOURNAL

FORGIVENESS JOURNAL

FORGIVENESS JOURNAL

FORGIVENESS JOURNAL

FORGIVENESS JOURNAL

FORGIVENESS JOURNAL

FORGIVENESS JOURNAL

Follow

Sent2Heal

On

Social Media

www.sent2heal.org
Shontefoster@Sent2heal.Org